The ABC

LONDON'S

II.—TRAMS &

by

S. L. POOLE

(Photo : S. L. Poole

An eight-feet-wide trolleybus of Class **SA3** *on service in Ilford.*

LONDON:

Ian Allan Ltd

1948

Photo : S. A. Newman

*A **J3** at work. Trolleybus No. 1039 operating Route 653, from Tottenham Court Road to Aldgate.*

The ABC of

LONDON'S TRANSPORT

PART II.—TRAMS & TROLLEYBUSES

INTRODUCTION

This is the second volume of the second edition of the A.B.C. of London Transport vehicles and deals with trams and trolleybuses.

The numerical lists of tramcars and trolleybuses have been supplied by the Press and Publications Officer of the London Passenger Transport Board, to whom the author's sincere thanks are due for assistance given. Although London Transport has willingly supplied such information as was requested by the author, this acknowledgment in no way signifies that London Transport either sponsors publication or accepts responsibility for any opinion either expressed or implied.

The author's particular thanks are due to the Council of the Light Railway Transport League for assistance given and data supplied from this body's official records. It is to be regretted that so short accounts only can be given from the extensive data made available.

Thanks are also due to the individual members of the League and to Mr. R. Elliott for assistance so promptly and generously given.

To Mr. Maurice Storr, who has supplied much information from his own personal records and observations, and has arranged for the tramway section to be approved by the Light Railway Transport League, I am most sincerely grateful.

Any note or observations on vehicles, sent to the author, c/o the Publishers, will be gratefully received and incorporated where applicable in any further editions.

S. L. POOLE.

LONDON, 1948.

INDEX

CHAPTER I

THE HISTORY OF LONDON'S TRAMWAYS

THE tramcar has probably been the cause of more discussion and controversy than any other unit of London's transport facilities. Its large passenger capacity and economical operating costs, coupled with extensive use by public authorities, made the tramcar a vital feature of public transport in the metropolis.

Tramway operation presented a different aspect of acquisition to the Board, for whereas buses, trains and trolleybuses were transferred from private companies and individuals, tramways were both publicly and privately owned.

London's tramways originated in a line built by an American engineer, George Francis Train, between Marble Arch and Notting Hill Gate, and opened to traffic on 23 March, 1861. The rails were taken up shortly after, the projecting rails being both a source of danger to other vehicles and provocative of legal troubles.

The first regular service was provided by the Metropolitan Street Tramways Company, which inaugurated a line between Brixton Station and Kennington Gate on 2 May, 1870. The North Metropolitan Tramways Company started a service between Whitechapel Church and Bow Church one week later. Both undertakings were subsequently acquired by the London County Council.

The London General Omnibus Co. Ltd., registered a subsidiary in 1860, under the name of the London Omnibus Tramways Co. Ltd., to operate a line from the Bank to Notting Hill Gate, but the scheme never materialised. Electric traction was inaugurated by the London United Tramways Co. Ltd., on 4 April, 1901, from Hammersmith and Shepherd's Bush to Kew Bridge, and Shepherd's Bush to Acton, although it has been stated officially that the last horse tram ran in London along the present route 70 until 1915, and Burdett Road was not converted to electric traction until after the 1914-18 war.

The following table gives details of the tramway undertakings in the year ending 31 March, 1933, which were transferred to the Board's ownership :—

Operator	Route miles operated	Car miles run on system	Cars owned	First Section opened
Public Authorities				
Bexley & Dartford	10.29	758,977	33	3 Oct., 1903
Croydon	9.28	2,272,746	55	9 „ 1879*
East Ham	8.34	1,991,963	56	
Erith	5.42	419,078	19	21 Aug., 1905
Ilford	7.13	1,203,300	40	March, 1903 (See text)
London County Council & Leyton Corporation	167.17	69,286,975	1,713	
Walthamstow	8.93	2,051,047	62	3 June, 1905
West Ham	16.27	4,094,859	134	(See text)
Companies :—				
Metropolitan Electric	53.51	12,603,503	316	22 July, 1904*
London United	29.05	5,180,390	150	(See text)
South Metropolitan	13.08	1,536,016	52	May, 1906

The first section of route of the County Borough of West Ham was opened by the North Metropolitan Tramways Company on 9 November, 1870, from Aldgate to Stratford Church, and the first electric line was from Stratford to the Abbey Arms, via Plaistow, opened on 27 February, 1904. On 22 June, 1901, the County Borough of East Ham commenced electrical working of the lines in its area, acquired from a company operator.

The London County Council was the largest operator in London, and its system was partly acquired from a number of companies and partly built by the Council itself. Eleven undertakings were purchased, in addition to some lines of the London United Tramways in the Hammersmith area (to form a link with sections of the Council's system in West London), and some sections (other than those mentioned below), from the Metropolitan Electric Tramways and Bexley U.D.C. These L.U.T. lines were acquired on 2 May, 1922. The Metropolitan Electric Tramways had previously sold to the Council, on 1 August 1912, the section of its undertaking between Finsbury Park and Manor House.

The Council also purchased the first regularly operated tramway routes in London, the Brixton-Kennington, and Whitechapel-Bow Church services already mentioned. The Council's operations began, however, on about 24 miles of route in South London, purchased from the London Tramways Company on 1 January, 1899.

*As Horse Tramway.

6

Leyton Corporation must also be considered with the London County Council. Leyton acquired horse tramways from the North Metropolitan Tramways and Lea Bridge, Leyton and Walthamstow Tramways Companies. Electric traction was inaugurated on the whole of the Leyton system on 1 December, 1906, and from 1 July, 1921, the lines were operated by the London County Council.

A special Act of Parliament of 1900 gave the Council powers to electrify its lines, and the first section to be so converted was that between the southern side of Westminster and Blackfriars Bridges, and Tooting, on 15 May, 1903. Thereafter electrification and the construction of extensions and new lines continued rapidly. It should be mentioned that the Highgate Village line was worked by cable traction before electrification by the Council.

When its undertaking was acquired by the Board, the London County Council operated a system of tramways far greater than the figures in the table, large though they may seem, would lead one to believe. Indeed, the London County Council's tramcars operated beyond the actual county boundary to the following points :—Purley, Wimbledon, Hampton Court (short period only), Mitcham, Hammersmith, Shepherd's Bush, North Finchley, Enfield, Edmonton, Chingford Mount, Epping Forest, Ilford, Barking. The Council's services did not penetrate the West End, however.

The Kingsway Tramway Subway, the only underground tramway route in London, links the tramway systems north and south of the Thames, via the Embankment. It was opened in February, 1906, as an isolated line from Bloomsbury to Aldwych, and on 10 April, 1908, was extended to join the then recently opened Embankment line at Waterloo Bridge.

At first, the subway was worked by special single deck cars of all metal construction, but in view of the importance of the North and South link, the Council decided to enlarge the tunnel to take double deck tramcars. It was therefore closed and supplanted by a special L.G.O.C. bus service along Kingsway itself on 3 February, 1930, and the alteration carried out mainly by lowering the floor of the tunnel. The route was reopened for the use of double deck tramcars on 15 January, 1931, from which date routes 31, 33 and 35 were worked to and from the suburbs on opposite sides of the river by tramcars of the E/3 design, a most serviceable vehicle which has proved very satisfactory in operation. To-day, 31, 33 and 35 are the last tram routes working in what may be called North London proper.

A feature of the L.C.C. tram working between 1913 and 1923 was the use of non-control, four wheel, open top, trailer cars, at first on the circular routes from Norbury to Norbury and Merton

7

to Merton (both via Embankment in two directions), the routes to Greenwich via Tower Bridge Road, Woolwich and Eltham, and Embankment, New Cross Gate Circular Routes.

Current for the L.C.C. tramways was supplied from its own power station at Greenwich, to which further reference is made In Part III of this ABC, which deals with railways.

In connection with the remainder of the public authorities, it may be mentioned that although the Tramways Act of 1870 empowered Local Authorities to purchase tramways, it did not authorise them to work the lines themselves, and in many cases authorities leased their lines to other operators. Leyton has already been mentioned in this respect and the tramways of the City of London Corporation, under a mile in all, were always leased to the London County Council.

Barking operated about a dozen trams of its own, which ran through to Aldgate during 1912 to 1914, but in February, 1929, the Barking Council abandoned the greater portion of its workings, which were assumed by Ilford, East Ham and L.C.C.

Dartford tramways had a varied history. At first they were worked by a private company, and then, after the original cars were destroyed by fire, by Bexley Council until 1921, when a Joint Committee with Bexley Council conducted operation with Bexley's own cars until acquisition by the Board.

The County Councils of Hertford and Middlesex leased all their lines, totalling of 1.50 and 42.63 miles respectively, to the Metropolitan Electric Tramways. Some M.E.T. cars bore on the sides the three sword device of the Middlesex County Council, and were lettered "Lessees of the Middlesex County Council."

The Underground group of companies did not allow itself to be left without an interest in tramway operation, and in 1928 acquired control of the following undertakings :—

> London United Tramways Ltd.
> Metropolitan Electric Tramways Ltd.
> South Metropolitan Electric Tramways & Lighting Co. Ltd.

Each of these companies had an interesting history, much of which concerns the development of its own particular area ; but again, it is with regret that only a brief outline can be given.

The London United system had it nucleus in the West Metropolitan Tramways Company Ltd., which in March, 1882, acquired a line in Acton from the Southall, Ealing and Shepherds Bush Tram Railway Company. London United operation as such began in August, 1894.

Inauguration of electric traction by the L.U.T. has been mentioned. For a number of years the Company had its own power station at Chiswick, but in August, 1917, current was taken from Lots Road, and the Chiswick station later became a sub-station.

Above: *The inauguration of electric traction on the London United Tramways, April,* 1901.
(*Photo*:
    London Transport

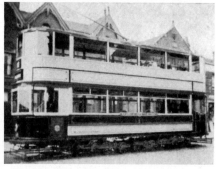

Right: *The County Borough of West Ham — a typical modern car* (*No.* 68).
(*Photo*: *R. Elliott*

Left: *East Ham Corporation Tramways car No.* 56, *with Brush body and trucks.*
(*Photo*: *R. Elliott*

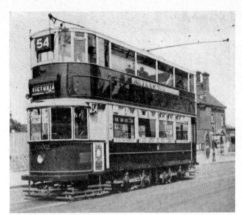

Left : A typical L.C.C. **E/3** car, with body by Hurst Nelson, trucks by E.M.B. and English Electric electrical equipment (No. 2002).

(Photo : R. Elliott

(Photo : R. Elliott

Walthamstow Corporation Tramways car No. 43. This vehicle was built in 1932 and transferred to the Board in 1933.

Metropolitan Electric Tramways originated in two routes : Finsbury Park Station to West Green Road, Tottenham, and Manor House to Wood Green, which were opened in sections for operation by horse trams between the years 1881 and 1885, and 1881 and 1887 respectively. These routes came under M.E.T. ownership on 13 January, 1902. The routes were at one time worked by the steam trams of the North London Steam Tramways Co. Ltd., which began in 1879 and were withdrawn in 1890 after being taken over by the North Metropolitan Tramways Co., who replaced the steam trams with two-horse trams.

The Company's first electrically worked section opened from Manor House on 22 July, 1904, and construction to Edmonton was completed on 24 August, 1905.

The first working under the agreement with the Middlesex County Council, which has been mentioned, was from Lordship Lane, Wood Green, to Bruce Grove, and was opened, electrically worked, on 20 August, 1904.

The bulk of the M.E.T. mileage was that leased from the Hertford and Middlesex County Councils and only 9.38 miles comprised the Company's own routes detailed above. Through running powers were granted to the L.C.C. over certain sections.

One of the best known routes of the M.E.T. was 19, from Tottenham Court Road to the country town of Barnet ; when the areas was converted to trolleybus operation it is to be regretted that route 19 simply vanished, its territory covered by sections of other services.

The Company is also notable in that with the London United, it introduced the modern Feltham, or U.C.C., type of car in 1931.

The South Metropolitan Electric Tramways and Lighting Company Ltd., opened its first sections of the Penge line, and the Croydon-Tooting, and Croydon-Sutton sections between May and December, 1906.

Hendon and Mitcham depots were used for overhauling rolling stock of all three companies, although the major portion of the London United work was done at Fulwell depot.

Sections of the systems detailed above, including large portions of the company-owned undertakings, have been converted since to trolleybus and motorbus operation. In the Annual Report for 1946, trams and trolleybuses are stated to cover 24% of the total mileage travelled by the Board's passengers, the journeys made by tram being 296,866,069.

At the outset of the Board's ownership, 2,630 tramcars passed to its control ; by the outbreak of war, the number had decreased to 1,255 ; and by December, 1946, to 913, with a total seating capacity of 65,832 persons. During the recent war, 69 tramcars were totally destroyed by enemy action, and the remainder damaged on 1,335 occasions.

In 1946, the Board stated that the remaining tramcar routes were to be converted to motor bus operation. The original intention had been to replace them with trolleybuses, but various factors altered this policy—although in view of the present position of deliveries, it is anticipated several years at least will elapse before the requisite motor buses can be obtained.

There is no doubt that a tramcar of modern design running on adequately maintained track is unequalled in its capacity to move large numbers of people speedily and economically from one point to another. But in London so many additional considerations have had to be taken into account, in view of the capital's peculiar population problems and future reconstruction schemes, that London Transport believe the advantages of the motorbus to outweigh those of the tramcar.

However excellent a tramway may be, its smoothness and efficient operation are seriously impaired when tracks have outlived their usefulness, have suffered from enemy action, and are still feeling the effects of the continuous wartime shortages of labour and material. The passing of tramcars of such proved serviceability as the Feltham E/3 and HR/2 classes will be regretted—to say nothing of the replacement of home produced fuel by imported motor fuel oil.

The Sunderland Corporation acquired the experimental Feltham type car No. 2168 with central entrance, and numbered it 100 in their fleet (of which it is the "show" car). There it is noted for its capacity to move large numbers of passengers quickly from one point to another. The car has been thoroughly overhauled, renovated, and fitted with the Corporation's modern type of pantograph current collection gear.

The Board envisaged a much speedier clearance of trams from its area, but various reasons caused a revision of the plan in 1937, and many of the existing tramcars were modernised and fitted with driver's vestibule screens.

The tramcar is unlike the motorbus in that its chassis, or frame, is not the work of one manufacturer. The most essential portion, the trucks, or bogies, are the work of specialist firms. The bodies are by a number of builders, in some cases the public authorities who owned the cars.

London tramcars are of the 8-wheeled type with two "maximum traction" bogies (except the HR/2 class), that is, bogies in which the weight of the car is brought to bear 65% on the driving wheels, 35% on the trailing or pony, thereby securing the maximum tractive effort. These bogies have one pair of large driving wheels, and a smaller pair of pony wheels to each truck. Two electric motors per tram are fitted (giving an average total h.p. of 120), driving the wheels through reduction gearing. The

HR/2 cars have equal sized wheels driving and four motors, one to each pair of wheels, giving a total h.p. of 140.

Brakes are of the magnetic track pattern, with the usual handbrake, but in the Feltham cars, compressed air braking is fitted in addition.

The two systems for the collection of electric current are familiar—the overhead wire, and the sub-surface conduit systems, the latter only within the London County Council area. As HR/2 cars Nos. 101 to 160 do not work beyond this area, they are still not fitted with trolley booms. London's first conduit tramway opened to the public was the Tooting line mentioned earlier.

London tramway routes to-day are worked with the following classes of car :—

(1) Class E/1.

A standard design of the London County Council, mounted on two maximum traction bogies. Seating capacity 78. Some cars are fitted with double trolley booms to obviate turning at termini.

Cars which have not been rebuilt have had their upper deck seats padded, but the seat backs are left wood slatted as before.

Windows on the top deck are wound up and down by rack and pinion.

Cars 552—601 inclusive are entirely new bodies, built in 1929, mounted on the old F and G class single deck car bogies, whereas the remainder of the E/1 cars are much older.

Some of the bodywork was by the London County Council themselves, others by Hurst Nelson & Co. Ltd., and the Brush Electrical Engineering Co. Ltd., with trucks by Hurst Nelson, Heenan and Froude, and Mountain & Gibson with a h.p. of 120.

(*i*) *Rehabilitated cars of the E/1 class. Marked "E1r" in the list following.*

The body sides have been built flush panelled externally to both decks. These cars have inset roller blind indicators for both route numbers and destination. New motors have been fitted, and the interior fittings modernised, on six of these cars.

(*ii*) *Marked "E1x" in the list following.*

This car has a more modern body with plywood roof and resembles Car No. 1 in external appearance.

(*iii*) *Marked "E1r xx" in the list following.*

As last described, with the usual turnover pattern seating.

(*iv*) *Marked "E1r xxx" in the list following.*

Early E-class body with rebuilt E/1 top deck.

(2) Class ME/3.

There were originally three of these cars, Nos. 1370 (rebuilt from M-class No. 1446), 1441 and 1444, and the construction was in all cases the same. "M" class car bodies were cut in two halves and a length spliced in the centre, making the bodies the same length as the standard E/1 cars. The only difference between the two classes is that the window spacing is unequal due to the fact that the corner pillars are 3ins. wider than the E/1 cars, the difference being made up in the centre windows which are an equal amount shorter. Trucks and electrical equipment are similar to the standard E/1 cars.

No. 1441 was destroyed by fire in 1944, 1370 on reconstruction had an entirely new top deck and is now classed by the Board as "Elr," while 1444 was fitted with the present wood constructed top cover after being damaged in a depot accident.

(3) Class E/3.

Metal bodied tramcars, with flush panelled sides to both decks, improved route number indicators of the metal stencil type, roller blind route indicators and half-drop, counter-balanced, sash windows on the upper deck.

The flush panelled sides to the lower deck allowed a wider gangway between the cross seats. Fifty bodies were built by the English Electric Co. Ltd., for Leyton, and 101 by Hurst Nelson for the L.C.C. The electrical equipment was by the English Electric Co. Ltd., and B.T.H.

The trucks were manufactured by the Electro-Magnetic Brake Co. Ltd., of West Bromwich, have roller bearing axles and a total h.p. of 115.

These cars have proved very serviceable, and, as is well known, maintain the Kingsway Subway services.

Car No. 1989 was built with the bucket pattern revolving seats.

(4) Class HR/2.

A development of the E/3 class for working hilly routes.

These cars have four motors, and the bogie wheels are of equal diameter. The trucks are by EMB, but vary in pattern.

The first fifty bodies were built by English Electric, the other fifty-nine by Hurst Nelson.

Cars Nos. 127 and 1893 suffered air raid damage at Camberwell Depot in 1940 and were reconstructed with rehabilitated top decks.

Three were sold to the Leeds Corporation in 1939. The numbers follow with the Leeds number in brackets after :—

Car No. 1881 (277) ;   1883 (278) ;   1886 (279)

(5) Class UCC (or "Feltham").

The most modern cars in London service, 54 being owned by the Metropolitan Electric Tramways Ltd., and 46 by the London United Tramways Ltd., which latter company placed the first car in service on 5 January, 1931.

A standard of comfort equal to that of the most modern bus was aimed at by the designers, coupled with all the undoubted advantages of electric traction.

These cars are 9ins. wider on the lower deck than the standard cars and lower in overall height. Transverse double seats are placed each side of the central gangway on the lower deck, as opposed to the general tramway practice typified by the L.C.C. E/3 class. There are no longitudinal seats on the lower deck.

The body is streamlined, and the trucks equipped with roller bearings, which give extremely smooth running. It was stated that the cars are so free in their running that they have been known to "coast" on roads always assumed to be dead level. For the first time, the driver was afforded the luxury of a totally enclosed cab, entered from within the body, and a driving seat.

These cars have power operated front exit doors, controlled by the driver, and there are double entrance doors at the rear, but the front door is now kept closed.

The seating capacity is 66, and is smaller than that of the L.C.C. E/3 class car, but the object was to provide more standing room, and to realise this, the vestibules were made spacious enough to accommodate 10 standing passengers in each, so that the saloon gangway was kept entirely clear. Thus the capacity of the car is 86, but 100 passengers are said to have been carried on special occasions such as football matches.

A staircase from each standing vestibule gives access to the upper deck, and a great advantage was that the conductor could collect his fares on the lower deck, mount the stairs, traverse the upper deck, and return to the entrance platform without any wasted walking on his part. Half drop windows are fitted to the upper deck.

Compressed air wheel and magnetic track brakes are provided. The handbrake is operated by a vertically placed wheel.

The cars were built by the Union Constructions and Finance Co. Ltd., of Feltham, hence the name "Feltham" by which they are known.

The Feltham cars entered service in 1931 in North and West London. To find suitable routes to use them to their best advantage was not easy, and the M.E.T. chose route 21, Holborn to North Finchley. For some years this had been worked by L.C.C. cars and route 29, Tottenham Court Road to Enfield, by the M.E.T. An exchange was arranged and the Feltham cars entered service on route 21. Later they also took over M.E.T. workings on 29, in conjunction with L.C.C. E/3 class cars.

The M.E.T. Feltham cars also worked M.E.T. route 40, and experimental car No. 2167, 39A, Enfield to Bruce Grove. The L.U.T. cars worked route 7, Shepherds Bush to Uxbridge, and on Sundays only, 55, Hanwell to Brentford.

With the conversion of the North and West London routes to trolleybus operation, the Feltham cars were transferred south, the ex-L.U.T. cars having to be fitted with plough collecting gear

15

for working on the conduit system.

In view of the length of the Felthams, Telford Avenue (Streatham Hill), depot had to be modified when they were transferred, but fortunately, the L.C.C. had erected a depot a few chains to the north of Christchurch Road, known as Brixton Hill, originally to accommodate the trailer cars.

In the early days of the war, several of the cars were laid up owing to the shortage of spare parts, and two at least (Nos. 2109 and 2113) were casualties from enemy action.

Before the Feltham class was evolved, there were a number of experimental cars, of which only one remains, No. 2167, which can be seen regularly and is distinguished by its low canopy and dashboard. This car proved successful in trials and was the basis of the design. The other experimental cars have now been sold or scrapped.

(6) Car No. 1.

Just before the formation of the Board, the London County Council built an experimental car, virtually a modernised version of the HR/2, of which there was to have been a number. Actually only one car was built, L.C.C. and London Transport No. 1, which was originally painted blue and became famous for the luxury of its appointments.

The body was built by the L.C.C. and the trucks were as for the HR/2 class. Air braking was fitted. The car is now classified as "HR/2 Experimental."

Car No. 1 has had a varied career since its transfer to the Board ; at first it was used on all-night service, and was last in the news on 15 May, 1938, when it worked a special journey for the Light Railway Transport League from Waltham Cross to Purley and back, the longest direct run ever made by a tramcar in London, approximately 28 miles each way. The car has been working regularly in the evenings recently.

(7) Classes WH, EH, K, CCT.

These cars came from West Ham, East Ham, Walthamstow, and Croydon Corporation Tramways, respectively, and are all similar to Class E/1. The Croydon Corporation cars had superior interior appointments such as blue upholstery and plated fittings. The cars differ in indicators and other details. Ex-West Ham cars 326, 327 and 330 are in service as staff cars. Bodywork varies as regards construction but the following are representative examples of the builders.:—

East Ham and West Ham Corporations, bodied by the Brush Electrical Engineering Co. Ltd. West Ham cars Nos. 295, 302, 331, 332, 333, 344, had bodies by the Corporation.

Cars 375 to 399 ex-Croydon were by Hurst Nelson.

Cars No. 2042 to 2053 ex-Walthamstow Corporation were built by Hurst Nelson and 2054 to 2061 by Brush.

NUMERICAL LIST OF TRAMCARS

NOTE.—The lists of numbers that follow must not be taken as an up-to-date and accurate schedule of vehicles currently in service. The are included expressly for the benefit of readers who like to note individual vehicles when seen; factual information on tramcars should be sought in the preceding text.

1 HR2Exp	126 HR2	173 E3	300 WH	393 CCT	590 El	1019 El
2 Elx	127 HR2	174 E3	301 WH	394 CCT	591 El	1022 Elr
81 EH	128 HR2	175 E3	302 WH	395 CCT	592 El	1024 Elr
82 EH	132 HR2	176 E3	304 WH	397 CCT	593 El	1025 El
83 EH	133 HR2	177 E3	305 WH	398 CCTEl	594 El	1030 El
84 EH	134 HR2	178 E3	306 WH	399 CCT	595 El	1032 El
85 EH	135 HR2	179 E3	307 WH	552 El	596 El	1033 Elr
86 EH	136 HR2	180 E3	308 WH	553 El	598 El	1038 El
87 EH	137 HR2	181 E3	309 WH	554 El	599 El	1042 Elr
88 EH	138 HR2	183 E2	310 WH	555 El	600 El	1049 El
89 EH	139 HR2	183 E3	311 WH	556 El	601 El	1050 El
90 EH	140 HR2	184 E3	312 WH	557 El	800 El	1059 El
91 EH	141 HR2	185 E3	331 WH	558 El	802 El	1076 El
92 EH	142 HR2	186 E3	332 WH	559 El	827 El	1077 El
93 EH	143 HR2	187 E3	333 WH	560 El	836 Elr	1079 El
94 EH	144 HR2	188 E3	334 WH	561 El	839 Elr	1083 El
95 EH	145 HR2	189 E3	335 WH	562 El	840 El	1087 Elr
96 EH	146 HR2	190 E3	336 WH	563 El	871 El	1088 Elr
97 EH	147 HR2	191 E3	337 WH	564 El	916 El	1089 Elr
98 EH	149 HR2	192 E3	338 WH	565 El	936 Elr	1090 Elr
99 EH	150 HR2	193 E3	339 WH	566 El	940 Elr	1092 El
100 EH	151 HR2	194 E3	340 WH	567 El	947 Elr	1094 El
101 HR2	152 HR2	195 E3	341 WH	568 El	948 Elr	1096 El
102 HR2	153 HR2	196 E3	342 WH	569 El	953 Elr	1103 Elrxx
103 HR2	154 HR2	197 E3	343 WH	570 El	955 El	1109 El
104 HR2	155 HR2	198 E3	344 WH	571 El	960 Elr	1128 El
105 HR2	156 HR2	199 E3	375 CCT	572 El	961 El	1137 El
106 HR2	157 HR2	200 E3	377 CCT	573 El	978 Elr	1139 El
107 HR2	158 HR2	201 E3	378 CCT	574 El	981 Elr	1140 El
108 HR2	159 HR2	202 E3	379 CCT Elr	575 El	982 Elrxx	1142 El
109 HR2	160 E3	203 E3	380 CCTElr	576 El	984 Elr	1143 El
110 HR2	161 E3	204 E3	381 CCT	577 El	985 Elr	1144 Elr-
111 HR2	162 E3	205 E3	382 CCT	578 El	993 El	1145 El
113 HR2	163 E3	206 E3	383 CCT	579 El	994 Elr	1149 El
114 HR2	164 E3	207 E3	384 CCT	580 El	995 Elr	1163 El
115 HR2	165 E3	208 E3	385 CCT	581 El	996 Elr	1165 El
116 HR2	166 E3	209 E3	386 CCT	582 El	1003 Elr	1170 El
117 HR2	167 E3	210 E3	387 CCT	584 El	1005 El	1171 El
118 HR2	168 E3	290 WH	388 CCT	585 El	1007 El	1172 El
119 HR2	169 E3	295 WH	389 CCT	585 El	1009 Elr	1174 El
120 HR2	170 E3	296 WH	390 CCT	587 El	1011 El	1175 El
121 HR2	171 E3	297 WH	391 CCT	588 El	1012 El	1177 Elr
122 HR2	172 E3	298 WH	392 CCT	589 El	1017 Elr	1182 El
		299 WH				

NUMERICAL LIST OF CARS—*continued.*

1187 El	1361 El	1486 El	1569 Elr	1644 El	1772 Elr	1835 El
1190 Elr	1362 El	1487 El	1570 El	1645 Elr	1773 El	1836 El
1191 Elr	1363 El	1488 El	1571 El	1646 El	1775 Elr	1837 El
1195 El	1364 Elr	1489 El	1572 Ele	1647 Elr	1777 El	1838 El
1204 El	1365 Elr	1491 Elr	1573 El	1648 Elr	1778 El	1839 El
1208 El	1366 El	1492 El	1574 Elr	1650 Ele	1779 El	1840 El
1211 El	1368 Elr	1493 El	1576 Elr	1651 El	1780 El	1841 El
1212 Elr	1369 Elr	1494 El	1577 Ele	1652 Elr	1781 El	1843 El
1213 El	1370 Elr	1495 El	1579 Elr	1653 El	1782 El	1844 El
1215 Elr	(late M E3)	1496 El	1581 El	1654 Elr	1783 El	1845 El
1216 Elr	1374 El	1497 El	1582 El	1655 El	1784 El	1846 El
1218 El	1375 Elr	1498 El	1587 El	1656 Elr	1785 El	1847 El
1219 El	1377 Elr	1499 El	1588 El	1657 El	1786 El	1848 El
1220 El	1378 El	1500 Elr	1589 El	1658 El	1787 El	1849 El
1223 El	1380 El	1501 El	1590 El	1659 El	1790 El	1850 El
1225 El	1381 Elr	1502 Elr	1592 El	1660 El	1791 El	1851 El
1226 Elr	1382 Elr	1503 El	1593 El	1661 Elr	1792 El	1854 HR2
1227 El	1383 El	1504 El	1594 El	1662 El	1793 El	1855 HR2
1229 El	1384 Elr	1506 Elr	1595 El	1663 El	1794 El	1856 HR2
1230 El	1385 Elr	1507 El	1596 E	1664 El	1795 El	1857 HR2
1321 El	1386 Elr	1508 Elr	1597Elxxx	1665 El	1796 El	1858 HR2
1233 El	1387 Elr	1514 El	1598 El	1666 El	1797 El	1859 HR2
1236 El	1388 Elr	1520 Elr	1599 Elr	1667 El	1798 El	1860 HR2
1238 El	1389 El	1525 El	1601 El	1668 Elr	1799 El	1861 HR2
1244 El	1390 El	1527 El	1602 El	1669 El	1800 El	1862 HR2
1246 Elr	1391 Elr	1529 El	1603 El	1670 El	1801 El	1863 HR2
1247 Elr	1392 Elr	1530 El	1604 El	1671 El	1802 El	1864 HR2
1248 Elr	1393 Elr	1531 El	1606 Elr	1672 El	1803 El	1866 HR2
1249 El	1395 El	1532 El	1608 El	1673 El	1804 El	1867 HR2
1250 El	1396 Elr	1533 El	1610 Elr	1674 El	1805 El	1868 HR2
1251 El	1397 Elr	1534 Elr	1611 El	1675 El	1806 El	1869 HR2
1252 El	1398 Elr	1537 El	1612 El	1676 Elr	1809 El	1870 HR2
1255 El	1399 Elr	1538 Elr	1613 El	1727 Elr	1810 El	1871 HR2
1260 Elrxx	1400 El	1540 El	1614 El	1728 El	1811 El	1872 HR2
1267 El	1401 Elr	1541 Elr	1617 El	1729 El	1812 El	1873 HR2
1270 El	1402 Elr	1542 El	1618 El	1730 Elr	1813 El	1874 HR2
1272 El	1404 El	1544 El	1619 Elr	1733 El	1814 El	1875 HR2
1275 Elr	1406 El	1545 Elr	1620 El	1743 Elr	1815 El	1876 HR2
1277 El	1407 El	1546 El	1621 El	1744 Elr	1817 El	1877 HR2
1291 El	1408 Elr	1547 Elr	1623 El	1749 El	1818 El	1878 HR2
1310 Elr	1409 El	1548 El	1624 El	1750 El	1819 El	1879 HR2
1312 El	1410 El	1549 El	1626 El	1753 El	1820 El	1880 HR2
1316 El	1413 El	1552 Elr	1627 El	1758 El	1822 El	1882 HR2
1317 El	1414 El	1555 El	1628 El	1760 El	1823 El	1884 HR2r
1332 El	1415 El	1557 El	1629 El	1761 Elr	1824 El	1885HR2r
1338 El	1419 El	1561 El	1630 El	1762 Elr	1926 El	1887HR2r
1350 El	1422 Elr	1562 El	1631 El	1673 El	1827 El	1888 HR2
1352 Elr	1423 El	1563 Elr	1636 Elr	1764 El	1828 El	1890HR2r
1353 Elr	1444 ME3	1564 Elr	1638 El	1766 Elr	1829 El	1891 HR2
1355 El	1478 El	1565 El	1640 El	1768 Elr	1830 El	1892 HR2
1357 Elr	1480 El	1566 Elr	1641 El	1769 Elr	1832 El	1893 HR2r
1358 El	1481 Elr	1567 El	1642 Elr	1770 Elr	1833 El	1894 HR2
1359 Elr	1485 El	1568 El	1643 Elr	1771 Elr	1834 El	1895 HR2

Right : M.E.T. type "G" car No. 233, with Brush body, M. & G. trucks and B.T.H. equipment. Built in 1908, the vehicle was fitted with a top cover by L.G.O.C. in 1929 Note the triangular eight-wheel brake sign.

Photo: R. Elliott

Left : A typical L.U.T. car. The vehicle is No. 269 of type **W1**

(Photo: R. Elliott

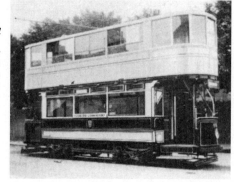

Right : Ilford Corporation Tramways car No. 40. This vehicle built in 1932, has since been sold to Sunderland Corporation.

(Photo: R. Elliott

2. *Class* **ME3.**

4. *Class* **HR2.**
Photos:
(W. J. Haynes

1. *Class* **E3**

3. *Class* **HR2**
(Rebuilt with
standard E1
top deck).

1896 HR2	1932 E3	1962 E3	2000 E3	2074 UCC	2104 UCC	2136 UCC
1897 HR2	1933 E3	1963 E3	2001 E3	2075 UCC	2105 UCC	2137 UCC
1904 E3	1934 E3	1964 E3	2002 E3	2076 UCC	2106 UCC	2138 UCC
1005 E3	1935 E3	1965 E3	2004 E3	2077 UCC	2107 UCC	2139 UCC
1906 E3	1936 E3	1966 E3	2042 K	2078 UCC	2108 UCC	2140 UCC
1907 E3	1937 E3	1968 E3	2043 K	2079 UCC	2110 UCC	2141 UCC
1908 E3	1938 E3	1969 E3	2045 K	2080 UCC	3111 UCC	2142 UCC
1909 E3	1939 E3	1970 E3	2046 K	2081 UCC	2112 UCC	2143 UCC
1910 E3	1940 E3	1971 E3	2047 K	2082 UCC	2114 UCC	2144 UCC
1911 E3	1941 E3	1974 E3	2048 K	2083 UCC	2115 UCC	2145 UCC
1912 E3	1942 E3	1975 E3	2049 K	2084 UCC	2116 UCC	2146 UCC
1913 E3	1943 E3	1977 E3	2050 K	2085 UCC	2117 UCC	2147 UCC
1914 E3	1944 E3	1979 E3	2052 K	2086 UCC	2118 UCC	2148 UCC
1915 E3	1945 E3	1980 E3	2053 K	2087 UCC	2119 UCC	2149 UCC
1916 E3	1946 E3	1981 E3	2054 K	2988 UCC	2120 UCC	2150 UCC
1917 E3	1947 E3	1984 E3	2055 K	2089 UCC	2121 UCC	2151 UCC
1918 E3	1948 E3	1986 E3	2056 K	2090 UCC	2122 UCC	2152 UCC
1919 E3	1949 E3	1987 E3	2057 K	2091 UCC	2123 UCC	2153 UCC
1920 E3	1950 E3	1988 E3	2058 K	2092 UCC	2124 UCC	2154 UCC
1921 E3	1951 E3	1989 E3	2059 K	2093 UCC	2125 UCC	2155 UCC
1922 E3	1952 E3	1990 E3	2060 K	2094 UCC	2126 UCC	2156 UCC
1923 E3	1953 E3	1991 E3	2061 K	2095 UCC	2127 UCC	2157 UCC
1924 E3	1954 E3	1992 E3	2066 UCC	2096 UCC	2128 UCC	2158 UCC
1925 E3	1955 E3	1993 E3	2067 UCC	2097 UCC	2129 UCC	2159 UCC
1926 E3	1956 E3	1994 E3	2068 UCC	2098 UCC	2130 UCC	2160 UCC
1927 E3	1957 E3	1995 E3	2069 UCC	2099 UCC	2131 UCC	2131 UCC
1928 E3	1958 E3	1996 E3	2070 UCC	2100 UCC	2132 UCC	2162 UCC
1929 E3	1959 E3	1997 E3	2071 UCC	2101 UCC	2133 UCC	2163 UCC
1930 E3	1960 E3	1998 E3	2072 UCC	2102 UCC	2134 UCC	2164 UCC
1931 E3	1961 E3	1999 E3	2073 UCC	2103 UCC	2135 UCC	2165 UCC
						2167 UCC

SERVICE VEHICLES.

In addition to the foregoing, there are a number of single decker 4-wheel tramcars which are used for maintenance purposes, e.g. stores, heavy wheel carriers, rail grinders and snowbrooms. Nos. 015 to 045 were reduced from double deckers, the remainder being specially built. In the snowbrooms, the body has been raised to enable the brush to be fitted underneath, and there is a dummy plough on the platform for clearing the ice and snow from the conduit slot.

All service cars in existence came from the London County Council, and a few still remain painted in L.C.C. maroon livery. A cypher is prefixed to the number of each of these cars, and the following is a list :—

Number	Trucks by	Purpose
02	Mountain & Gibson	Rail grinder
04	,,	,, ,,
05	Brill 21E	Stores van
06	,,	Stores van
08	Mountain & Gibson	Stores van
09	,,	Stores van

No.	Trucks by	Purpose
010	Mountain & Gibson	Stores van
011	,,	Wheel van
012	,,	,, ,,
014	Brill 21E	Railgrinder
015	,,	Stores van
016	,,	Snowbroom
017	,,	Snowbroom
018	,,	Snowbroom
019	,,	Snowbroom
010	,,	Snowbroom
021	,,	Snowbroom
022	,,	Snowbroom
023	,,	Snowbroom
024	,,	Snowbroom
025	,,	Snowbroom
026	,,	Snowbroom
028	,,	Snowbroom
029	,,	Snowbroom
031	,,	Snowbroom
032	,,	Snowbroom
033	,,	Snowbroom
034	,,	Snowbroom
035	,,	Snowbroom
036	,,	Snowbroom
037	,,	Snowbroom

TRAM DEPOTS.

Tram operation is conducted from a number of depots in South London, and one in North London (Holloway), which accommodates tramcars for working the Subway services, but is otherwise allocated to trolleybuses.

List of tramway depots is as follows :—

Abbey Wood.
Brixton Hill.
Camberwell.
Clapham.
Holloway (tram and trolleybus).
New Cross.
Norwood.
Purley (Storage depot).
Streatham, Telford Avenue.
Thornton Heath.
Wandsworth (tram and trolleybus).

The Central Repair depot for all tramcars is at Charlton, S.E. where trolleybuses are also overhauled as detailed under the trolleybus section.

CHAPTER II

TROLLEYBUSES

Trolleybuses assumed considerable importance during the ten years before the recent war, and they are now a major factor in London's transport facilities. During 1946, trolleybuses carried 889,178,391 passengers in the London area.

Trolley vehicles made their appearance late in the last century in Germany, in the form of single decker cars with two motors driving the rear wheels, either through chains or directly, in which case the motors were mounted actually in the wheel hubs.

To combine the flexibility of the rubber tyred motor bus with all the benefits of electric traction has been a much desired union, but difficulties were experienced in providing for the current return, which is normally available through tramway rails.

The type of vehicle known to-day as the trolleybus was the subject of experiment as early as 1899. The first demonstration in London occurred in 1909, when on the 25 September, the "first British-built Railless Trolley Car," to quote a contemporary journal, was built and equipped for experimental running on a road specially prepared by the Metropolitan Electric Tramways Ltd., in its Hendon depot. Although this vehicle bore the destination boards Golders Green Station—The Burroughs, Hendon, it ran within the depot only and was not operated on public service.

The first British trolleybuses to run in public service were at Leeds and Bradford, both of which independently started a trolleybus service on the same day in June, 1911. Rotherham Corporation inaugurated services on 3 October, 1912, and this municipality's system has developed into one of the most successful of the British undertakings.

Another experimental installation, inaugurated in Hove, had the Cedes-Stoll current collecting equipment, of Austrian manufacture. A light four-wheeled trolley with grooved wheels ran on overhead wires, and was connected by a flexible cable or rope to the vehicle itself, together with two electrical connecting cables. This particular vehicle only ran for a very short while, but other operators used the same system of current collection, and the name "trolleyvehicle" was derived from the overhead trolley described. In 1914, six Cedes-Stoll vehicles were imported from Austria and put to work at Keighley, in Yorkshire, where they ran until 1921.

Increasing attention to trolleybuses was the more urgent because of the question of tramway replacement. This was a very pressing problem as, largely owing to neglect during the 1914-18 war, the track of most systems needed replacement, in addition to new tramcars. Large outlays of capital expenditure had been made on power stations and overhead systems of current distribution, and to supersede all this by motor buses meant a large write-off, or at least a serious depreciation of the assets. In addition, electric traction possessed many undoubted advantages.

Naturally the trolleybus, which combined much of the mobility of the motor bus with the ability to use power from existing sources, received more and more attention as improvements were made in body design and equipment, including foot pedal control of power, single motor installation, shaft transmission and pneumatic tyres. A further advantage of the trolleybus over the motor bus was its greater ease of control ; it could therefore be driven by tram drivers who were elderly, or otherwise not adaptable to training in handling a motor bus with its clutch and gearbox.

Between 1921 and 1937, trolleybus route mileage outside the metropolis was extended from 47 to 445, and the number of vehicles increased from 80 to 1559. In most instances, the new vehicles replaced tramways, but some new routes were opened as well.

Trolleybuses were first publicly operated in the London area on 16 May, 1931, when London United Tramways Ltd. converted approximately one mile of tramway from Twickenham Junction to Teddington Station, completed conversion of tramways in the Kingston, Twickenham, Teddington and Wimbledon areas, which are now trolleybus routes 601, 602, 603, 604, and added certain extensions by 2 September, 1931, amounting to 17.26 miles.

The fleet of 60 trolleybuses put into service had 6-wheel A.E.C. chassis, with single 80 h.p. motors under the bonnets. Electrical equipment was supplied for the first 35 by English Electric Co. Ltd., the remainder by British Thomson-Houston Co. Ltd.

The bodies seated 56 and were of composite wood and metal construction, built by the Union Construction & Finance Co. Ltd., of Feltham. The trolleybus bodies resembled the LT bus in appearance in some respects and were largely to the pattern of the builders' "Feltham" tramcar bodies.

. Current collection was by wheel trolleyheads as fitted to tramcars, and the overhead noise was excessive. There was also a good deal of "drumming" on the top deck roof.

The traction circuit was not earthed, as in a tramcar, and this caused considerable interference to radio reception in the vicinity. A special vehicle with test apparatus circulated in the affected areas, and as a result, choking coils were evolved for the suppression of interfrence. These coils were fitted one in front of each trolley arm on the roof, and are now standard fittings.

The Board decided that replacement of the whole of the London trams was essential, and parliamentary powers were obtained for conversion. In the New Works Programme of 1935, provision was made for conversion from tram to trolleybus operation of 148 miles, in addition to conversions already in hand. Parliamentary Acts of 1936 and 1937 authorised conversion of a further 52½ route miles and on 31 December, 1946, the position was that trolleybuses operated on 224 miles of converted tramway route, 31 miles of other route, and that authority existed for a further 100 route miles.

Experiments were conducted to determine the best type of trolleybus for production in numbers. Due regard had to be paid to the question of seating capacity, which in the trams averaged 74, as against 70 in the standard trolleybus. Therefore, to carry the same number of passengers, a slightly more frequent trolleybus service was called for, which involved, alternatively, a greater daily mileage per trolleybus, or a larger trolleybus fleet pro rata to the trams displaced.

A standard vehicle was evolved, and with the exception of one single unit, the Board's present fleet is mounted on 6-wheel chassis, produced by the Associated Equipment Co. Ltd., or Leyland Motors Ltd., the product of each manufacturer being identical in all major characteristics.

The standard model body is of all-metal construction, with rear entrance, and seats 70. Trolleybuses Nos. 385 to 483 seat 69, and the special short wheelbase vehicles, Nos. 64 to 181, and 484 to 493, seat 60.

In buses numbered between 64 and 493 inclusive, a longitudinal seat was projected into the nearside of the driver's compartment, accompanied by a notice requesting passengers not to talk to the driver. The vehicles were not long in being in this form, and were altered to allow the now customary full width driver's compartment, isolated from the body by a glazed bulkhead. In this compartment, the driver sits in the normal offside position, and the rest of the space is used for controls and electrical equipment.

The standard trolleybus is equipped with a single compound wound motor of 95 h.p. operating at 550 volts direct current. The motor is placed amidships beneath the floorboards, driving both rear axles through short shafts. The laden weight of the vehicle is 13¼ tons.

The bodies are of all-metal construction, so that low voltage lighting is compulsory, and double banks of batteries, with a capacity of 45 amperes hours are installed, which not only supply current for lighting, but are able to propel the vehicle at 4 m.p.h. in emergency. A motor-driven generator, operating at line voltage, automatically recharges the batteries. A great advantage of battery lighting is that the vehicle remains lighted when for any reason line current is interrupted.

The original L.U.T. trolleybuses of 1931 were equipped with vacuum assisted brakes, but this was superseded by compressed air and electrical braking on later standard trolleybuses. The electrical braking system takes advantage of the fact that when the electric motor is rotated by the continuing momentum of the trolleybus, an electric current is produced. By the upward movement of the power pedal this regenerated current is returned to the supply line.

When speed is reduced to a point at which current cannot be returned to the line, initial movement of the brake pedal operates the rheostatic brake, in which this regenerated current is induced to form a powerful resistance to continued turning of the motor. The life of the ordinary friction brake linings has been found to be so considerably increased that it is obvious much of the braking is done by the electrical system. The ordinary bus pattern handbrake is also provided to hold the trolleybus at rest.

The adoption of a full width driver's compartment has been mentioned. The additional space so gained permitted the control gear to be removed from positions about the chassis to this compartment, where it is more accessible and protected.

Control is very simple ; the driver is seated in the normal position, with the steering wheel facing him, the power pedal to his left, the brake pedal and handbrake lever to his right. Slightly to the right, above his eye level, is the dewirement indicator, a neon tube which glows as long as the trolleys are "on" the overhead wire and picking up current. On the driver's left is the air brake emergency signal.

Immediately pressure in the system falls below the safe working minimum of 50lbs. per square inch, a red flag bearing the word "STOP" rises and a buzzer sounds continuously. The vehicle is then taken out of service for examination.

Beside and below the driver's seat is a handle which controls the motor for working in forward or reverse.

The control resistances, which are cut in and out of circuit by contactors, are placed beneath the floor, and cooled by the current of air admitted through the opening in the front of the vehicle.

Trolley noise has been eliminated by the use of sliding shoe current pick-up with carbon insets, but regular lubrication of the overhead wires is necessary to prevent abnormal wear. Special vans have been built for the purpose and mounted on motorbus chassis. These vans have two trolley booms, each of which carries at its upper extremity a lubricant box filled with colloidal graphite. This is conveyed to the overhead conductor by a grooved trolleywheel, which is partly submerged in the lubricant box. Wear on the conductor wire is said to be negligible, while dewirements are very infrequent.

Experiments have been continuing to enable the driver to change the direction of the frogs in the overhead wire from his cab, instead of the task having to be done by the conductor from the kerb. An electrical induction device is fitted, with a delayed action switch, so that the driver can select his course through busy junctions, and devote his whole attention to driving. One trolleybus (90) at Sutton is fitted with the apparatus.

One experimental trolleybus, Class X5, No. 1379, has rear entrances on both sides for working through Kingsway subway, where the central station platforms require offside loading facilities. The decision to operate motor buses negatives the experiment and the trolleybus operates normally.

A four-wheel-steering trolleybus, with only one rear axle, No. 1671, is in regular service.

Production of "chassisless" vehicles was in progress in 1939, and there is also a design in which the body is carried on outriggers from the chassis. The advantages of these types of construction are decreased weight and overall height, and improved disposition of the electrical equipment.

Generally, London trolleybuses are of a likeness in all but constructional details. The A.E.C. chassis can be distinguished from the Leyland by the fact that the former has polished metal covers to the rear hubs, with the A.E.C. trademark in colours thereon. The Leyland has dark metal hub caps with "Leyland" embossed thereon. Electrical equipment is by one of the specialist firms.

At the outbreak of war, the Board had 1,469 trolleybuses, but by 31 December, 1946, this number had increased to 1,747, with a total seating capacity of 120,675, including 43 intended for operation in South Africa. It was not possible to ship these latter overseas, so they were transferred to the Board for operation.

The bodies intended for use abroad, although of the same general outline, vary considerably in detail construction, and were, for the first time in England, 8ft. wide. This increased width is considered to be so beneficial for working that more vehicles of the same width are on order.

During the war, 15 trolleybuses were destroyed, and the remainder damaged on 1,527 occasions. 77 new trolleybuses were ordered at the beginning of 1946. These are for immediate delivery and are of the latest pattern with 8 ft. wide bodies,.

27

18 trolleybuses with front exits were borrowed from the Bournemouth Corporation during the war, and were used in the Ilford area. Painted bright yellow, with a maroon waist band, the standard Bournemouth Corporation livery, these were Sunbeam-B.T.H. vehicles, used for the first time in London.

Vehicles on the Highgate Hill (611), and Sutton-Crystal Palace (654) routes, have special braking arrangements, and are controlled to a maximum speed of 2 m.p.h. in reverse, thereby obviating the danger of run back on the very steep hills traversed.

Registration numbers of all standard trolleybuses accord with the stock number; thus trolleybus 926 has the registration number of ELB 926. 1001 and over have only the end figures of the registration number in accord with the stock number.

Trolleybuses are allocated to 21 depots, 19 of them converted from tramway operation, and two combined tram and trolleybus (Holloway and Wandsworth).

All trolleybus routes are numbered in the 500 or 600 series, and in many instances, the route number has been created by the addition of 500 or 600 to the old tramway route number.

The class of each trolleybus is always displayed inside the back platform wall beneath the window.

─────────

The following abbreviations are used in connection with the vehicles :—

Chassis:

AS   A.E.C. standard 6-wheel chassis.
AS4 ,,   ,,   4-wheel   ,,
ASE A.E.C. earlier 6-wheel chassis as fitted to L.U.T. vehicles
AC   A.E.C. 6-wheel chassisless construction.
LS   Leyland standard 6-wheel chassis.
LC   Leyland 6-wheel chassisless construction.
LFS Leyland experimental 4-wheel steering 6-wheel chassis.

Bodywork:

B	Brush Electrical Engineering Co. Ltd.
BRCW	Birmingham Railway Carriage & Wagon Co. Ltd.
EE	English Electric Co. Ltd.
LM	Leyland Motors Ltd.
LGO	London General Omnibus Co. Ltd.
LT	London Passenger Transport Board.
MCW	Metropolitan-Cammell-Weymann Motor Bodies Ltd.
PR	Park Royal Coachworks Ltd.
UCC	Union Construction & Finance Co. Ltd.

General

A	Vehicle damaged in air raid and rebuilt as standard type.
X	Experimental vehicle.

1. The original **E1** class.

2. Rebuilt **E1** class.

3. The pride of the L.C.C. Tramways —Car No. 1.

4. The only remaining Experimental "Feltham" (No. 2167).

(Photos: W. J. Haynes

Class **HR/2,** *with trolley booms (Car No. 1887). The destination blind and route number have also been modified.*

Photos: W. J. Haynes

Class **HR/2** *with top deck from E1 Class car (Car No. 127) Compare trucks with those of Car No. 1887 above.*

Right : An ex-West Ham tramcar in the service of the Board (Class **WH**)

Left : An ex-Walthamstow Corporation tramcar on service 27, before the latter's conversion to trolleybus operation.

(*Photos : Author*

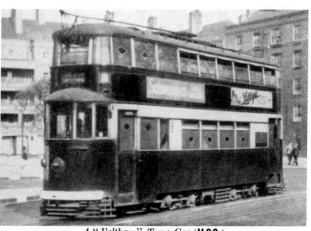

*A " Feltham " Type Car (***UCC.***)*

(*Photo: J. W. Haynes*

*Left : Snowplough
No. 020, with H R2
type car following.*

*Right : A bus
chassis converted to
a conduit cleaner
(Vehicle No.113W).*

*An E1 type car at a changeover to conduit current collection. Note
the plough collectors.*

Photos: W. J. Haynes

Numerical List of Trolleybuses

Class A.1 CHASSIS : ASE
Ex. L.U.T. BODY : UCC
56 SEATS.

1	13	25
2	14	26
3	15	27
4	16	28
5	17	29
6	18	30
7	19	31
8	20	32
9	21	33
10	22	34
11	23	35
12	24	

Class A.2 CHASSIS : ASE
Ex. L.U.T. BODY : UCC
56 SEATS.

36	44	52
37	45	53
38	46	54
39	47	55
40	48	56
41	49	57
42	50	58
43	51	59
		60

Class X.1 CHASSIS : ASE
Ex. L.U.T. BODY : LGO
74 SEATS
Central Entrance.
61

Class X.2 CHASSIS : ASE
BODY : MCW
62

Class X.3 CHASSIS : AS4
BODY : EE
63

Class B.1 CHASSIS : LS
Short Type BODY : B
for use on BODY : BRCW
hilly routes.

64	68	72	76
65	69	73	77
66	70	74	78
67	71	75	79

80	93	106	119
81	94	107	120
82	95	108	121
83	96	109	122
84	97	110	123
85	98	111	124
86	99	112	125
87	100	113	126
88	101	114	127
89	102	115	128
90	103	116	129
91	104	117	130
92	105	118	131

Class C.1 CHASSIS : AS
BODY : MCW

132	145	158	171
133	146	159	172
134	147	160	173
135	148	161	174
136	149	162	175
137	150	163	176
138	151	164	177
139	152	165	178
140	153	166	179
141	154	167	180
142	155	168	181
143	156	169	182
144	157	170	183

Class C.2 CHASSIS : AS
BODY : MCW

184	209	234	259
185	210	235	260
186	211	236	261
187	212	237	262
188	213	238	263
189	214	239	264
190	215	240	265
191	216	241	266
192	217	242	267
193	218	243	268
194	219	244	269
195	220	245	270
196	221	246	271
197	222	247	272
198	223	248	273
199	224	249	274
200	225	250	275
201	226	251	276
202	227	252	277
203	228	253	278
204	229	254	279
205	230	255	280
206	231	256	281
207	232	257	282
208	233	258	283

Class C.3   CHASSIS : AS   BODY : BRCW

284	309	334	359
285	310	335	360
286	311	336	361
287	312	337	362
288	313	338	363
289	314	339	364
290	315	340	365
291	316	341	366
292	317	342	367
293	318	343	368
294	319	344	369
295	320	345	370
296	321	346	371
297	322	347	372
298	323	348	373
299	324	349	374
300	325	350	375
301	326	351	376
302	327	352	377
303	328	353	378
304	329	354	379
305	330	355	380
306	331	356	381
307	332	357	382
308	333	358	383

Class D.1   CHASSIS : LS   BODY : LM

384

Class D.2   CHASSIS : LS   BODY : LM

385	410	435	460
386	411	436	461
387	412	437	462
388	413	438	463
389	414	439	464
390	415	440	465
391	416	441	466
392	417	442	467
393	418	443	468
394	419	444	469
395	420	445	470
396	421	446	471
397	422	447	472
398	423	448	473
399	424	449	474
400	425	450	475
401	426	451	476
402	427	452	477
403	428	453	478
404	429	454	479
405	430	455	480
406	431	456	481
407	432	457	482
408	433	458	483
409	434	459	

Class B.3   CHASSIS : LS

Short type as BODY : B

484	485	486	487
			488

Class B.2   CHASSIS : LS   BODY : BRCW

489	505	521	537
490	506	522	538
491	507	523	539
492	508	524	540
493	509	525	541
494	510	526	542
495	511	527	543
496	512	528	544
497	513	529	545
498	514	530	546
499	515	531	547
500	516	532	548
501	517	533	549
502	518	534	550
503	519	535	551
504	520	536	552
			553

Class E.1   CHASSIS : AS   BODY : B

554	566	578	591
555	567	579	592A
556	568	580	593
557	569	581	594
558	570	582	595
559	571	583	596
560	572	584	597
561	573	585	598
562	574	586	599
563	575	587	600
564	576	588	601
565	577	589	602
		590	603

Class E.2   CHASSIS : AS   BODY : PR

604	610	616	622
605	611	617	623
606	612	618	624
607	613	619	625
608	614	620	626
609	615	631A	627
			628

Class E.3   CHASSIS : AS   BODY : MCW

629	635	641	647
630	636	642	648
631	637	643	649
632	638	644	650
633	639	645	651
634	640	646	652
			653

Class F.1 — CHASSIS: LS — BODY: MCW

654	679	704	729
655	680	705	730
656	681	706	731
657	682	707	732
658	683	708	733
659	684	709	734
660	685	710	735
661	686	711	736
662	687	712	737
663	688	713	738
664	689	714	739
665	690·	715	740
666	691	716	741
667	692	717	742
668	693	718	743
669	694	719	744
670	695	720	745
671	696	721	746
672	697	722	747
673	698	723	748
674	699	724	749
675	700	725	750
676	701	726	751
677	702	727	752
678	703	728	753

Class X.4 — CHASSIS: AC — Front Door — BODY: LT
Normal rear entrance platform.

754

Class H.1 — CHASSIS: LS — BODY: MCW

755	779	803	827
756	780	,804	828
757	781	805	928
758	782	806	830
759	783	807	831
760	784	808	832
761	785	809	833
762	786	810	834
763	787	811	835
764	788	812	836
765	789	813	837
766	790	814	838
767	791	815	839
768	792·	816	840
769	793	817	841
770	794	818	842
771	795	819	843
772	796	820	844
773	797	821	845
774	798	822	846
775	799	823	847
776	800	824	848
777	801	825	849
778	802	826	850

851	864	877	891
852	865	878	892
853	866	879	893
854	867	880	894
855	868	881	895
856	869	882	896
857	870	883	897
858	871	884	898
859	872	885	899
860	873	886	900
861	874	887	901
862	875	888	902
863	876	889	903
		890	904

Class J.1 — CHASSIS: AS — BODY: MCW

905	917	929	941
906	918	930	942
907	919	931	943
908	920	932	944
909	921	933	945
910	922	934	946
911	923	935	947
912	924	936	948
913	922	937	949
914	926	928	950
915	927	939	951
916	928	940	952

Class L.1 — CHASSIS: AS — BODY: MCW

953

Class L.2 — CHASSIS: AS — BODY: MCW

954

Class J.2 — CHASSIS: AS — BODY: MCW

955	974	993	1012
956	975	994	1013
957	976	995	1014
958	977	996	1015
959	978	997	1016
960	979	998	1017
961	980	999	1018
962	981	1000	1019
963	982	1001A	1020
964	983	1002	1021
965	984	1003	1022
936	985	1005	1023
967	986	1005	1024
968	987	1006	1025
969	988	1007	1026
970	989	1008	1027
971	990	1009	1028
972	991	1010	1029
973	992	1011	

Class J.3 — CHASSIS : AS — BODY : BRCW

1030	1036	1042	1048
1031	1037	1043	1049
1032	1038	1044	1050
1033	1039	1045	1051
1034	1040	1046	1052
1035	1041	1047	1053
			1054

Class K.1 — CHASSIS : LS — BODY : LM

1055	1080	1105	1130
1056	1081	1106	1131
1057	1082	1107A	1132
1058	1083	1108	1133
1059	1084	1109	1134
1060	1085	1100	1135
1061	1086	1111	1136
1062	1087	1112	1137
1063	1088	1113	1138
1064	1089	1114	1139
1065	1090	1115	1140
1066	1091	1116	1141
1067	1092	1117	1142
1068	1093	1118	1143
1069	1094	1119	1144
1070	1095	1120	1145
1071	1096	1121	1146
1072	1097	1122	1147
1073	1098	1123A	1148
1074	1099	1124	1149
1075	1100	1125	1150
1076	1101	1126	1151
1077	1102	1127	1152
1078	1103	1128	1153
1079	1104	1129	

Class K.2 — CHASSIS : LS — BODY : LM

1154	1175	1196	1217
1155	1176	1197	1218
1156	1177	1198	1219
1157	1178	1199	1220
1158	1179	1200	1221
1159	1180	1201	1222
1160	1181	1202	1223
1161	1182	1203	1224
1162	1183	1204	1225
1163	1184	1205	1226
1164	1185	1206	1227
1165	1186	1207	1228
1166	1187	1208	1229
1167	1188	1209	1230
1168	1189	1210	1231
1169	1190	1211	1232
1170	1191	1212	1233
1171	1192	1213	1234
1172	1193	1214	1235
1173	1194	1215	1236
1174	1195	1216	1237
1238	1242	1246	1250
1239	1243	1247A	1251
1240	1244	1248	1252
1241	1245	1249	1253

Class K.1 — CHASSIS : LS — BODY : LM

1254	1267	1280	1293
1255	1268	1281	1294
1256	1269	1282	1295
1257	1270	1283	1296
1258	1271	1284	1297
1259	1272	1285	1298
1260	1273	1286	1299
1261	1274	1287	1300
1262	1275	1288	1301
1262	1276	1289	1302
1264	1277	1290	1303
1265	1278	1291	1304
1266	1279	1292	

Class K.2 — CHASSIS : LS — BODY : LM

1305	1318	1331	1344
1306	1319	1332	1345
1307	1320	1333	1346
1308	1231	1334	1347
1309	1322	1335	1348
1310	1323	1336	1349
1311	1323	1337	1350
1312	1325	1338	1351
1313	1326	1339	1253
1314	1327	1340	1353
1315	1328	1341	1354
1316	1329	1342	
1317	1330	1343	

Class L.1 — CHASSIS : AC — BODY : MCW

1355	1359	1363	1367
1356	1360	1364	1368
1357	1361	1365	1369
1358	1362	1366	

Class L.2 — CHASSIS : AC — BODY : MCW

1370	1372	1374	1376
1371	1373	1375	1377
			1378

Class X.5 — CHASSIS : AC — BODY : LT

Designed for working through Kingsway Subway. Entrance on both sides at rear.

1379

Class L.3 CHASSIS : AC BODY : MCW

1380	1417	1454	1491
1381	1418	1455	1492
1382	1419	1456	1493
1383	1420	1457	1494
1384	1421	1458	1495
1385	1422	1459	1496
1386	1423	1460	1500
1387	1424	1461	1501
1388	1425	1462	1502
1389	1426	1463	1503
1390	1427	1464	1504
1391	1428	1465	1505
1392	1429	1466	1506
1393	1430	1467	1507
1394	1431	1468	1508
1395	1432	1469	1509
1396	1433	1470	1510
1397	1434	1471	1511
1398	1435	1472	1512
1399	1436	1473	1513
1400	1437	1474	1514
1401	1438	1475	1515
1402	1439	1476	1516
1403	1440	1477	1517
1404	1441	1478	1518
1405	1442	1479	1519
1406	1443	1480	1520
1407	1444	1481	1521
1408	1445	1482	1522
1409	1446	1483	1523
1410	1447	1484	1524
1411	1448	1485	1525
1412	1449	1486	1526
1413	1450	1487	1527
1414	1451	1488	1528
1415	1452	1489	1529
1416	1453	1490	

Class M.1 CHASSIS : AC BODY : LT

1530	1536	1542	1548
1531	1537	1453	1549
1532	1538	1544	1550
1533	1539	1545	1551
1534	1540	1546	1552
1535	1541	1547	1553
			1554

Class N.1 CHASSIS : AS BODY : BRCW

1555	1563	1571	1579
1556	1564	1572	1580
1557	1565	1573	1581
1558	1566	1574	1582
1559	1567	1575	1583
1560	1568	1576	1584
1561	1569	1577	1585
1562	1570	1578,	1586

1587	1602	1617	1632
1588	1603	1618	1633
1589	1604	1619	1634
1590	1605	1620	1635
1591	1606	1621	1636
1592	1607	1622	1637
1593	1608	1623	1638
1594	1609	1624	1639
1595	1610	1625	1640
1596	1611	1626	1641
1597	1612	1627	1642
1598	1613	1628	1643
1599	1614	1629	1644
1600	1615	1630	
1601	1616	1631	

Class N.2 CHASSIS : AS BODY : PR

1645	1651	1658	1664
1646	1652	1659	1665
1647	1653	1660	1666
1648	1654	1661	1667
1649	1656	1662	1668
1650	1657	1663	1669

Class X.6 CHASSIS : AC BODY : EE

1670

Class X.7 CHASSIS : LFS BODY : LM

1671

Class K.3 CHASSIS : LS BODY : LM

1672	1678	1684	1690
1673	1679	1685	1691
1674	1680	1686	1692
1675	1681	1687	1693
1676	1682	1688	1694
1677	1683	1689	1695
			1696

Class P.1 CHASSIS : LS BODY : MCW

1697	1705	1711	1717
1700	1706	1712	1718
1701	1707	1713	1719
1702	1708	1714	1720
1703	1709	1715	1721
1704	1710	1716	

1722-1764
Class SA.1 CHASSIS : LS

This Class and Classes SA.2 and S.A.3 were intended for use in South Africa and have 8ft. wide bodies.

1722	1725	1728	1731
1723	1726	1729	1732
1724	1727	1730	1733

Class SA.2 CHASSIS : LS

1734	1737	1740	1743
1735	1738	1741	1744
1736	1739	1742	1745
			1746

Class SA.3 CHASSIS : AS

1747	1752	1757	1762
1748	1753	1758	1762
1749	1754	1759	1764
1750	1755	1760	
1751	1756	1761	

TROLLEYBUS DEPOTS.

Bexley Heath.
Bow.
Edmonton.
Fulwell.
Hackney.
Hammersmith.
Hanwell.
Hendon.
Holloway (trolleybus and tram).
Hounslow.
Ilford.
Leyton.
North Finchley.
Poplar.
Stamford Hill.
Stonebridge Park.
Sutton.
Walthamstow.
Wandsworth (trolleybus and tram).
West Ham.
Wood Green.

Trams and trolleybuses carry a duty number only (on the lower deck waist line), and, unlike the motor buses. the depots have no code.

The Central Repair Depot, Charlton, overhauls trolleybuses from the North Eastern and South Eastern areas; it supplies all units for trolleybuses. Fulwell and West Ham each have works attached in which trolleybuses are overhauled.

TRAM AND TROLLEYBUS ROUTES
TRAMS

Route No.	Terminal Points	Route
2.	WIMBLEDON STATION—VICTORIA EMBANKMENT (WESTMINSTER BRIDGE)	South Wimbledon Merton Tooting Balham Clapham Kennington **Returns via Blackfriars Bridge and Elephant and Castle**
4.	WIMBLEDON STATION—VICTORIA EMBANKMENT (BLACKFRIARS BRIDGE)	South Wimbledon Merton Tooting Balham Clapham Kennington **Returns via Westminster Bridge**
6.	TOOTING (AMEN CORNER)—CITY (SOUTHWARK)	Balham Clapham Common Stockwell Kennington Elephant and Castle Southwark Bridge
8.	TOOTING—VICTORIA STATION	Southcroft Road Mitcham Lane Streatham Brixton Stockwell South Lambeth Road **Returns as Route 20**
20.	VICTORIA STATION—TOOTING	Vauxhall Bridge Road South Lambeth Road Stockwell Clapham Balham
10.	TOOTING BROADWAY—CITY (SOUTHWARK)	Southcroft Road Mitcham Lane Streatham Brixton Kennington Elephant and Castle Southwark Bridge
12.	WANDSWORTH (HIGH STREET)—LONDON BRIDGE (BOROUGH)	York Road Battersea Nine Elms Lane Vauxhall Lambeth Road Southwark Bridge Road
16.	PURLEY—VICTORIA EMBANKMENT	Croydon Norbury Streatham Brixton Kennington Westminster Bridge **Returns via Blackfriars Bridge Elephant and Castle**

Route No.	Terminal Points	Route
18.	PURLEY—VICTORIA EMBANKMENT	Croydon Norbury Streatham Brixton Kennington Elephant and Castle Blackfriars Bridge **Returns via Westminster Bridge**
22.	TOOTING—VICTORIA EMBANKMENT	Southcroft Road Mitcham Lane Streatham Brixton Stockwell South Lambeth Road Albert Embankment Westminster Bridge Victoria Embankment **Returns as Route 24**
24.	VICTORIA EMBANKMENT—TOOTING	Victoria Embankment Westminster Bridge Albert Embankment South Lambeth Road Stockwell Clapham Balham
26.	CLAPHAM JUNCTION—LONDON BRIDGE (BOROUGH)	Lavender Hill Wandsworth Road Vauxhall Westminster Bridge Embankment Blackfriars Bridge Southwark Street
28.	CLAPHAM JUNCTION—VICTORIA STATION	Lavender Hill Wandsworth Road Vauxhall Bridge Road
31.	BATTERSEA (PRINCES HEAD)—WESTMINSTER—BLOOMSBURY*	Nine Elms Vauxhall Albert Embankment Westminster Bridge Kingsway Subway
33.	WEST NORWOOD—FINSBURY PARK (MANOR HOUSE STN.)	Herne Hill Brixton Kennington Westminster Bridge Kingsway Subway Bloomsbury Angel Essex Road Green Lanes
34	CHELSEA (KINGS ROAD)—BLACKFRIARS**	Battersea Bridge Falcon Road Clapham Junction Lavender Hill Clapham Common Stockwell Road Brixton Coldharbour Lane Camberwell Green Elephant and Castle Blackfriars Road

*Service extended to Bloomsbury in peak hours only.
** Alternate trams operate to Camberwell Green only at certain hours.

The inauguration of London's first service trolleybuses, at Teddington, 1931. The picture shows London United Tramways' vehicles, which became the Board's "A" Class.

Photo: A.E.C. Ltd.

The experimental trolley vehicle tested by Metropolitan Electric Tramways Ltd. in 1909.

The first large capacity trolleybus—the 64-seater of the London United Tramways Ltd.

(*Photos: London Transport*

Route No.	Terminal Points	Route
35.	FOREST HILL—HIGHGATE (ARCHWAY STN.)	Brockley Rise Crofton Park Brockley Station New Cross Peckham Camberwell Green Elephant and Castle Westminster Bridge Victoria Embankment Kingsway Subway Bloomsbury Angel Upper Street, Highbury Holloway
36.	ABBEY WOOD—VICTORIA EMBANKMENT	Woolwich Charlton Greenwich New Cross Old Kent Road New Kent Road Elephant and Castle Blackfriars Bridge **Returning via Westminster Bridge**
38.	ABBEY WOOD—VICTORIA EMBANKMENT	Woolwich Charlton Greenwich New Cross Old Kent Road New Kent Road Elephant and Castle Westminster Bridge **Returning via Blackfriars Bridge**
40.	PLUMSTEAD (WICKHAM LANE)*— WOOLWICH (BERESFORD SQUARE) VICTORIA EMBANKMENT (SAVOY STREET)	Charlton Greenwich Deptford New Cross Peckham Camberwell Green Kennington Westminster Bridge
42.	CROYDON (COOMBE ROAD)— THORNTON HEATH	Croydon High Street London Road Brigstock Road Thornton Heath High St.
44.	WOOLWICH (BERESFORD SQUARE) —ELTHAM	Academy Road Well Hall Road
46.	WOOLWICH (BERESFORD SQUARE) —CITY(SOUTHWARK)	Academy Road Well Hall Road Eltham High Street Lee Green Lewisham New Cross Old Kent Road Great Dover Street Southwark Bridge

Extended to Wickham Lane in weekday peak hours.

48

Route No.	Terminal Points	Route
48.	WEST NORWOOD—CITY (SOUTHWARK)	Herne Hill Milkwood Road Coldharbour Lane Camberwell Green Elephant and Castle Southwark Bridge Road
52.	GROVE PARK STATION—CITY (SOUTHWARK)	Downham Estate Bromley Road Catford Lewisham New Cross Old Kent Road Great Dover Street Southwark Bridge
54.	GROVE PARK STATION—VICTORIA STATION	Downham Estate Bromley Road Catford Lewisham New Cross Peckham Camberwell Green Kennington Vauxhall Bridge
56.	PECKHAM RYE—VICTORIA EMBANKMENT	East Dulwich Denmark Hill Camberwell Green Elephant and Castle Westminster Bridge **Return via** **Blackfriars B'ge (weekdays)** **Westminster B'ge (Sundays)**
58.	BLACKWALL TUNNEL—VICTORIA STATION	Blackwall Lane Greenwich South Street Lewisham Rushey Green Catford Forest Hill Dulwich Dog Kennel Hill Camberwell Green Kennington Vauxhall Bridge
60.	DULWICH LIBRARY—CITY (SOUTHWARK)	Denmark Hill Camberwell Green Elephant and Castle Southwark Bridge
62.	FOREST HILL—VICTORIA EMBANKMENT (SAVOY STREET)	Dulwich Dog Kennel Hill Camberwell Green Elephant and Castle Westminster Bridge
66.	FOREST HILL—VICTORIA STATION	Crofton Park Brockley New Cross Peckham Camberwell Green Kennington **Vauxhall Bridge**

Route No.	Terminal Points	Route
68.	GREENWICH CHURCH—WATERLOO STATION	Deptford Rotherhithe Bermondsey Tower Bridge Road New Kent Road Elephant and Castle London Road
70.	GREENWICH CHURCH—LONDON BRIDGE STATION	Deptford Rotherhithe Bermondsey Tooley Street
72.	WOOLWICH (BERESFORD SQUARE) —NEW CROSS—VICTORIA EMBANKMENT* (SAVOY STREET)	Academy Road Westhorne Avenue Lee Lewisham New Cross Peckham Camberwell Green Kennington Westminster Bridge
74.	GROVE PARK STATION**—DOWN-HAM (BROMLEY ROAD)— BLACK-FRIARS	Catford Forest Hill Crofton Park Brockley New Cross Old Kent Road New Kent Road Elephant and Castle Blackfriars Road
78.	WEST NORWOOD—VICTORIA STATION	Tulse Hill Herne Hill Effra Road Brixton Stockwell Vauxhall Bridge Road
84.	***PECKHAM RYE—VICTORIA EMBANKMENT	East Dulwich Denmark Hill Camberwell Green Elephant and Castle Blackfriars Bridge **Return via** **Westminster Bridge**

* *Extended to Victoria in weekday peak hours only.*
** *Extended to Grove Park Station on Saturday afternoons and Sundays only.*
*** *Weekdays only.*

45

ALL NIGHT TRAMS
(Saturday Nights Excepted)

Route No.	Terminal Points	Route
1.	TOOTING & TOOTING (CIRCLE)	Streatham Brixton Westminster Blackfriars Brixton Streatham **or** Balham Clapham Blackfriars Westminster Clapham Balham
3.	BATTERSEA—BLACKFRIARS	Battersea Park Road Nine Elms Lane Vauxhall Westminster Bridge
5.	DOWNHAM (BROMLEY ROAD)—VICTORIA EMBANKMENT (SAVOY STREET)	Catford Lewisham New Cross Gate Old Kent Road Elephant and Castle Blackfriars Bridge
7.	NEW CROSS GATE—VICTORIA EMBANKMENT (SAVOY STREET)	Camberwell Green Elephant and Castle Blackfriars Bridge
26.	CLAPHAM JUNCTION—LONDON BRIDGE	Lavender Hill Wandsworth Road Vauxhall Westminster Blackfriars
35.	HIGHGATE (ARCHWAY STN.)—WESTMINSTER STN.	Holloway Road Upper Street Rosebery Avenue Theobalds Road Kingsway Subway

TROLLEYBUS ROUTES

Route No.	Terminal Points	Route
513.	HAMPSTEAD—HOLBORN CIRCUS PARLIAMENT HILL FIELDS *(weekdays only)*	Royal College Street Pancras Road Grays Inn Road Holborn Farringdon Road Pancras Road Royal College Street Kentish Town Road
517.	NORTH FINCHLEY—HOLBORN CIRCUS	Highgate Road East Finchley Archway Road Highgate Holloway Caledonian Road Kings Cross Grays Inn Road **Returning via Farringdon Road**
521.	NORTH FINCHLEY—HOLBORN CIRCUS	New Southgate Wood Green Manor House Finsbury Park Seven Sisters Road Caledonian Road Kings Cross Grays Inn Road **Returning via Farringdon Road**
543.	WOOD GREEN STATION (L.T.)—HOLBORN CIRCUS	Lordship Lane Bruce Grove Stamford Hill Stoke Newington Kingsland Road Shoreditch Old Street Clerkenwell Road Grays Inn Road **Returning via Farringdon Road**
555.	WOODFORD*—LEYTON GREEN—BLOOMSBURY	Leyton High Road Lea Bridge Road Clapton Hackney Cambridge Heath Shoreditch Old Street Clerkenwell Road
557.	CHINGFORD MOUNT—LIVERPOOL STREET STATION	Chingford Road Hoe Street Lea Bridge Road Clapton Hackney Cambridge Heath Shoreditch

Service extended to Woodford on Sundays only.

Route No.	Terminal Points	Route
565.	BARKING — HOLBORN CIRCUS	London Road Barking Road East India Dock Road Commercial Road Commercial Street Gt. Eastern Street Old Street Clerkenwell Road Grays Inn Road
567.	BARKING—ALDGATE—SMITHFIELD	London Road Barking Road East India Dock Road Commercial Road Aldgate High St. (*Sunday*) Commercial Street Great Eastern Steret Old Street Clerkenwell Road St. John Street
569.	NORTH WOOLWICH—ALDGATE	Pier Road Albert Road North Woolwich Road Silvertown Way East India Dock Road Commercial Road Aldgate High Street
581.	WOODFORD (NAPIER ARMS)—BLOOMSBURY	Woodford New Road Whipps Cross Lea Bridge Road Clapton Hackney Dalston Essex Road Rosebery Avenue Theobalds Road
601.	TOLWORTH (KINGSTON BY-PASS)—TWICKENHAM	Ewell Road St. Mark's Hill Claremont Road Penrhyn Road Eden Street Kingston Bridge Hampton Wick Teddington Broad Street Stanley Road
602.	DITTONS—KINGSTON HILL LOOP—DITTONS	Portsmouth Road Brighton Road Victoria Road Claremont Road Penrhyn Road Eden Street London Road Park Road Kings Road Richmond Road Eden Street Penrhyn Road Claremont Road Victoria Road Brighton Road Portsmouth Road

Route No.	Terminal Points	Route
603.	TOLWORTH ("RED LION")— KINGSTON HILL LOOP— TOLWORTH	Ewell Road St. Marks Hill Claremont Road Penrhyn Road Eden Street Richmond Road Kings Road Park Road London Road Eden Street Penrhyn Road Claremont Road St. Marks Hill Ewell Road
604.	HAMPTON COURT—WIMBLEDON STATION	Kingston Bridge Clarence Street Norbiton Cambridge Road Kingston Road Malden West Barnes Raynes Park Worple Road Broad Street
605.	TEDDINGTON—NEW MALDEN— WIMBLEDON*	Teddington High Street Ferry Road Kingston Road Upper Teddington Road Hampton Wick High Street Kingston Bridge Clarence Street Norbiton Cambridge Road Kingston Road Malden West Barnes Lane Worple Road
607.	UXBRIDGE—SHEPHERDS BUSH	Hillingdon Hayes Southall Hanwell Ealing Acton Uxbridge Road
609.	BARNET—MOORGATE	Great North Road North Finchley High Road East Finchley Archway Road Highgate Holloway Highbury Angel City Road
611.	HIGHGATE VILLAGE—MOORGATE	Highgate Hill Highgate Holloway Highbury New North Road East Road City Road

*Service extended to Wimbledon in peak hours only

Route No.	Terminal Points	Route
612.	MITCHAM (FAIR GREEN)—BATTERSEA (PRINCES HEAD)	London Road Tooting Broadway Garratt Lane York Road
613.	PARLIAMENT HILL FIELDS—HOLBORN CIRCUS—HAMPSTEAD	Highgate Road Kentish Town Road Royal College Street Pancras Road Farringdon Road Holborn Grays Inn Road Pancras Road Royal College Street
617.	NORTH FINCHLEY—HOLBORN CIRCUS	East Finchley Archway Road Highgate Holloway Caledonian Road Kings Cross Farringdon Road **Returning via Grays Inn Road**
621.	NORTH FINCHLEY—HOLBORN CIRCUS	New Southgate Wood Green Manor House Finsbury Park Seven Sisters Road Caledonian Road Kings Cross Farringdon Road **Returning via Grays Inn Road**
615.	PARLIAMENT HILL FIELDS—MOORGATE	Kentish Town Camden Town Royal College Street Pancras Road Kings Cross Angel City Road
623.	WOODFORD (NAPIER ARMS)—MANOR HOUSE STATION	Woodford New Road Forest Road Ferry Lane Seven Sisters Road
625.	WOODFORD—WOOD GREEN—WALTHAMSTOW (BECONTREE AVE.)—WINCHMORE HILL *Weekday peak hours only*	Woodford New Road Forest Road Tottenham Hale Bruce Grove Lordship Lane Green Lanes Walthamstow (Becontree Avenue)* Winchmore Hill*
626.	ACTON (MARKET PLACE)—CLAPHAM JUNCTION	Horn Lane Harlesden Scrubs Lane Shepherds Bush Hammersmith Fulham Palace Road Putney Bridge Wandsworth High Street

Trolleybus No. 63, the only four-wheel unit in the Board's fleet.

Trolleybus No. 62, the prototype of the Board's 70-seat vehicles.
Note the longitudinal seat beside the driver's compartment.

(*Photos : London Transport*)

(Photo : London Transport

Trolleybus No. 754, embodying chassisless construction and with front exit. The body was built at Charlton.

(Photo : W. J. Haynes

Experimental type **X7** *vehicle, with four-wheel steering.*

Route No.	Terminal Points	Route
627.	PONDERS END*—EDMONTON TOWN HALL—TOTTENHAM COURT RD.	Hertford Road New Road Fore Street High Road Tottenham Seven Sisters Road Manor House Finsbury Park Holloway Camden Town Hampstead Road
628.	CRAVEN PARK—CLAPHAM JUNCTION ; HARROW ROAD— CLAPHAM JUNCTION (Sundays only)	Harlesden Scrubs Lane Shepherds Bush Hammersmith Fulham Palace Road Putney Bridge Wandsworth High Street
629.	ENFIELD TOWN—TOTTENHAM COURT ROAD	Winchmore Hill Wood Green Finsbury Park Camden Town
630.	HARROW ROAD (SCRUBS LANE)— W. CROYDON STATION	Scrubs Lane Shepherds Bush Hammersmith Putney Bridge Wandsworth Garratt Lane Tooting Mitcham Common Tamworth Road
639.	HAMPSTEAD—MOORGATE	Camden Town Crowndale Road Kings Cross Angel City Road
641.	WINCHMORE HILL—MOORGATE	Wood Green Manor House Southgate Road New North Road
643.	WOOD GREEN STATION (L.T.)— HOLBORN CIRCUS	Lordship Lane Bruce Grove Stamford Hill Stoke Newington Kingsland Road Shoreditch Old Street Clerkenwell Road Farringdon Road **Returning via Grays Inn Road**
645.	BARNET—CANONS PARK	North Finchley Church End Golders Green Cricklewood Hendon Colindale Edgware

Service extended to Ponders End in morning peak hours only.

Route No.	Terminal Points	Route
647.	STAMFORD HILL—LONDON DOCKS	Stoke Newington Dalston Kingsland Road Shoreditch Commercial Street Leman Street
649.	WALTHAM CROSS*—PONDERS END—LIVERPOOL STREET STATION	Hertford Road Edmonton Tottenham High Road Stamford Hill Stoke Newington Dalston Kingsland Road
653.	ALDGATE—TOTTENHAM COURT ROAD	Whitechapel Road Mile End Gate Cambridge Heath Hackney Clapton Stamford Hill Amhurst Park Manor House Finsbury Park Holloway Camden Town
654.	SUTTON (BUSHEY ROAD)—CRYSTAL PALACE	Benhill Avenue Carshalton Road Wallington Tamworth Road West Croydon Northcote Road Selhurst Anerley
655.	ACTON—HANWELL DEPOT—HAMMERSMITH— CLAPHAM JUNCTION**	Uxbridge Road Ealing Broadway Boston Road Brentford Half Acre Chiswick High Road Kings Street Putney Bridge Wandsworth
657.	HOUNSLOW—SHEPHERDS BUSH	Isleworth Brentford Kew Chiswick Goldhawk Road
659.	WALTHAM CROSS—HOLBORN CIRCUS	Ponders End Edmonton Tottenham Seven Sisters Road Manor House Finsbury Park Holloway Caledonian Road Kings Cross

*Service extended to Waltham Cross on
   Sundays only.
**Service extended to Acton (Market Place)
   and certain journeys to Acton (Bromyard Avenue) and to
   Clapham Junction during weekday peak hours only.

Route No.	Terminal Points	Route
660.	NORTH FINCHLEY—HAMMER-SMITH	Church End Golders Green Cricklewood Willesden Craven Park Harlesden Horn Lane Acton Vale Askew Road
661.	LEYTON (L.T. DEPOT)—ALDGATE	Whipps Cross Leytonstone Stratford Bow Mile End Whitechapel
662.	SUDBURY—PADDINGTON GREEN	Wembley Stonebridge Park Craven Park Harlesden Kensal Green Harrow Road
663.	ILFORD BROADWAY—ALDGATE	Manor Park Forest Gate Stratford Bow Mile End Whitechapel
664.	EDGWARE (STATION ROAD)—PADDINGTON GREEN	Colindale Hendon Cricklewood Willesden Craven Park Harlesden Kensal Green Harrow Road
665.	BARKING BROADWAY—BLOOMS-BURY	East Ham Plaistow Canning Town Poplar Aldgate
666.	EDGWARE (STATION ROAD)—HAMMERSMITH	Colindale Hendon Cricklewood Willesden Craven Park Harlesden Horn Lane Acton Vale Askew Road
667.	HAMPTON COURT—HAMMERSMITH	Hampton Fulwell Twickenham Isleworth Brentford Kew Chiswick Turnham Green Youngs Corner King Street

Route No.	Terminal Points	Route
669.	STRATFORD BROADWAY—NORTH WOOLWICH	West Ham Lane Plaistow Station Upper Road Hermit Road Barking Road Silvertown Way North Woolwich Road
677.	WEST INDIA DOCKS—SMITHFIELD	Burdett Road Mile End Victoria Park Hackney Dalston Essex Road Goswell Road Clerkenwell Road St. John Street
679.	WALTHAM CROSS—SMITHFIELD	Ponders End Edmonton Tottenham Seven Sisters Road Manor House Finsbury Park Holloway Highbury Upper Street Angel St. John Street
683.	STAMFORD HILL—MOORGATE	Dalston Balls Pond Road Southgate Road East Road
685.	WALTHAMSTOW (CROOKED BILLET) —CANNING TOWN*	Billet Road Mark House Road Church Road Leyton High Road Crownfield Road Wanstead Flats Woodgrange Road Romford Road Green Street Barking Road Billet Road
687.	WALTHAMSTOW**—LEYTON— VICTORIA & ALBERT DOCKS	Markhouse Road Church Road Leyton High Road Crownfield Road Woodgrange Road Upton Lane Stopford Road Plaistow High Street Balaam Street New Barn Street

*Service extended to Silvertown Station
weekday peak hours and Sunday afternoons.
**Service extended to Walthamstow in
weekday peak hours only.

Route No.	Terminal Points	Route	
689 and 690	STRATFORD BROADWAY—EAST HAM TOWN HALL—STRATFORD BROADWAY	689/690	West Ham Lane Church Street Plashet Lane
		689	Plashet Grove High St. North Barking Road Green Street
		690	Green Street High St. North Plashet Grove
		689/690	Plashet Road Portway Church Street West Ham Lane
691.	BARKINGSIDE—BARKING BROADWAY		Horns Road Ley Street Ilford Ilford Lane
693.	CHADWELL HEATH—BARKING BROADWAY		Goodmayes Seven Kings High Road Ilford Ilford Lane
695	CHADWELL HEATH—BOW CHURCH		Ilford Romford Road Stratford Broadway Bow
696.	WOOLWICH (FREE FERRY)—DARTFORD (MARKET STREET)		Plumstead Wickham Lane Welling Bexleyheath Dover Road Crayford West Hill
697.	CHINGFORD MOUNT—VICTORIA & ALBERT DOCKS		Chingford Road Hoe Street Leyton High Street Crownfield Road Leytonstone Road Stratford Broadway Plaistow Road Plaistow High Street Balaam Street New Barn Street
698.	WOOLWICH (FREE FERRY)—BEXLEYHEATH		Plumstead Abbey Wood Belvedere Erith Bexley Road Erith Road May Place Road
699.	CHINGFORD MOUNT—VICTORIA & ALBERT DOCKS		Chingford Road Hoe Road Leyton High Street Crownfield Road Leytonstone Road Stratford Broadway Plaistow Road Plaistow High Street Greengate Street Prince Regent Lane

ALL NIGHT TROLLEYBUSES
(Saturday Nights Excepted)

Route No.	Terminal Points	Route
513 and 613.	HAMPSTEAD—HOLBORN CIRCUS	Kentish Town Royal College Street Pancras Road Kings Cross
543 and 643.	STAMFORD HILL—HOLBORN CIRCUS	Stoke Newington Shoreditch Old Street Clerkenwell Road
612.	MITCHAM—BATTERSEA (PRINCES HEAD)	London Road Mitcham Road Garratt Lane York Road
628.	HAMMERSMITH—CLAPHAM JUNCTION	Fulham Palace Road Putney Bridge High Street Wandsworth
665.	POPLAR (BLACKWALL TUNNEL)—BLOOMSBURY	East India Dock Road Commercial Road Shoreditch Great Eastern Street Old Street Clerkenwell Road

A Bournemouth Corporation Sunbeam trolleybus at work in Ilford on the Board's Barkingside-Barking service, February, 1941.

(Photo: C. F. Klapper)

*A Class **J1** trolleybus, with A.E.C. chassis and M.C.W. body-work, at work on service 621.*

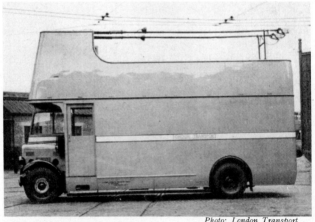

Photo: London Transport

One of the specially constructed overhead wire lubricating vehicles, mounted on an A.E.C. bus chassis.

NOTES

NOTES

First published 1948
Reprinted 2000

ISBN 0 7110 2760 9

Published by Ian Allan Publishing

an imprint of Ian Allan Publishing Ltd, Terminal House, Station Approach, Shepperton,
Surrey TW17 8AS.

Printed by Ian Allan Printing Ltd, Riverdene Business Park, Hersham, Surrey KT12 4RG.

Code: 0005/A

This is a facsimilie reprint of an original edition first published in 1948 and as such all
advertisements, with the exception of inside front and back covers and rear cover are no
longer valid.